"Use your success, wealth and influence to put them in the best position to realize their own dreams and find their true purpose."

-Kobe Bryant

The New Cypher Publishing
Chicago, Illinois
thenewcypher@gmail.com

Books Published by Jim Blissitt III
are published under the auspices of
The New Cypher Spoken Word Charter, LLC

© 2021 by Jim Blissitt III
All rights reserved
Printed in the United States of America

Written by Jim Blissitt III
Illustrated by Manuel Nieto

Text design and composition by Jim Blissitt III

Library of Congress Cataloging-in-Publication Data
Blissitt III, Jim
Whatever Happened to the Boy Who Played Basketball All Night?

36 Pages
ISBN 9780578674704 (hardback)

WHATEVER HAPPENED TO THE BOY WHO PLAYED BASKETBALL ALL NIGHT?

Written by Jim Blissitt III
Illustrated by Manuel Nieto

The New Cypher Publishing

*Dedicated to the most active students of
Freedom School.*

A Special thanks to Jim Blissitt Jr., Stephen Howard, Michael McKenzie Jr., Terrence Carter, Micah Crawford, Lynette Dancy, Simuel Hampton, Adrian Durry, Gregory Rodgers, Sandra Elmore, Michael Miles, Anterio Jackson, Ana-Alisa Guthrie, Chloe Lewis, Leslie Gueno, Laura Demby-Blissitt, Christopher Griffith, Wanda Blissitt

You stood with me before everyone else.

Jump Shots from the corner, layups from the left and the right...

His mother flew across oceans...

He sometimes felt sad because his father also left when he was a boy.

Whatever happened to the boy who played basketball all night?

He imagined his dad grabbed the rebound as his mother cheered from the crowd.

Taking shot after shot, he found, helped him smile whenever he frowned.

Whatever happened to the boy who played basketball all night?

He always imagined his father was a king far away.

You must be smart to be a prince...

Math, science, reading and art... he studied before basketball would start.

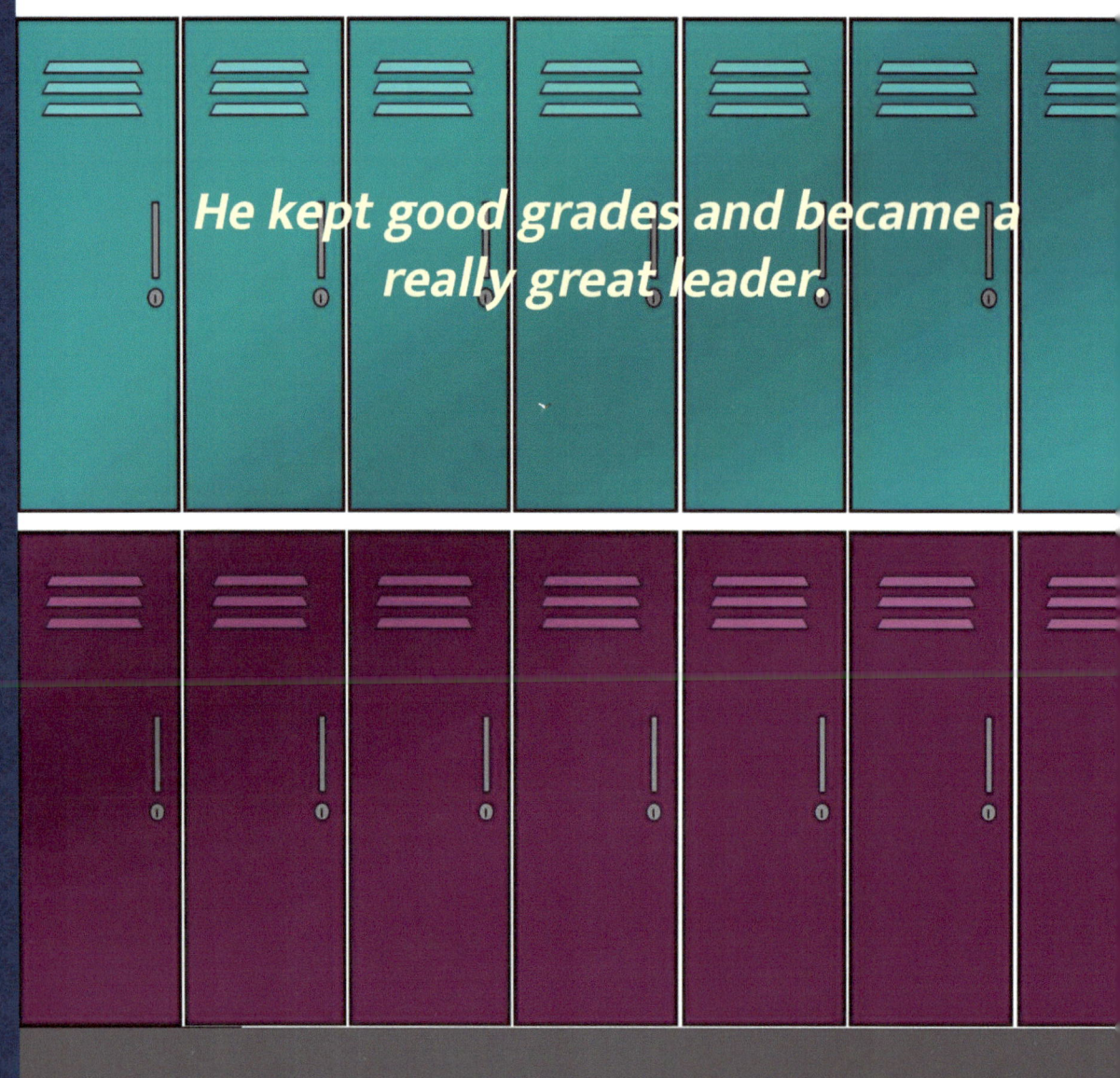

He kept good grades and became a really great leader.

He was not only good at defense, off the court he was also great as a reader.

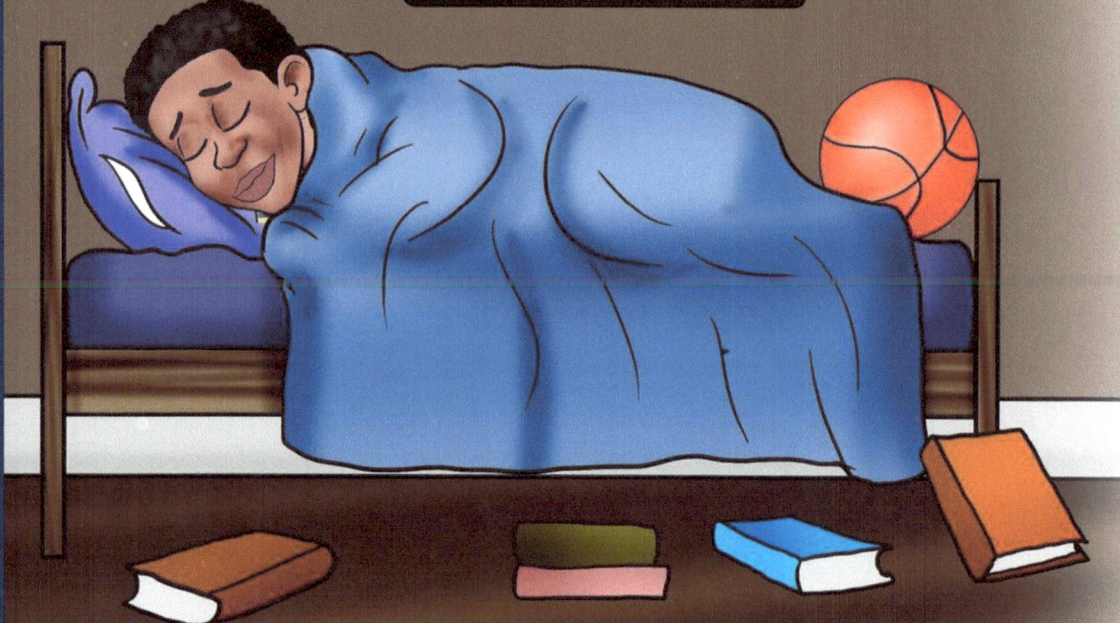

Basketball kept him healthy and gave him all the tools...

He taught about hope and wanted everyone to be equal.

and became the 44th President of the United States.

www.ingramcontent.com/pod-product-compliance
Lightning Source LLC
Chambersburg PA
CBHW041411160426
42811CB00106B/1633